It's a Thunderstorm!

by **Nadia Higgins**

illustrated by **Damian Ward**

Content Consultant: Steven A. Ackerman
Professor of Atmospheric Science
University of Wisconsin-Madison

Weather Watchers

magic Wagon

visit us at www.abdopublishing.com

Published by Magic Wagon, a division of the ABDO Group, 8000 West 78th Street, Edina, Minnesota 55439. Copyright © 2010 by Abdo Consulting Group, Inc. International copyrights reserved in all countries. All rights reserved. No part of this book may be reproduced in any form without written permission from the publisher.

Looking Glass Library™ is a trademark and logo of Magic Wagon.

Printed in the United States of America, North Mankato, Minnesota.
092009
012010

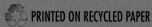 PRINTED ON RECYCLED PAPER

Text by Nadia Higgins
Illustrations by Damian Ward
Edited by Mari Kesselring
Interior layout and design by Nicole Brecke
Cover design by Becky Daum

Library of Congress Cataloging-in-Publication Data
Higgins, Nadia.
  It's a thunderstorm! / by Nadia Higgins ; illustrated by Damian Ward ; content consultant, Steven A. Ackerman.
      p. cm. — (Weather watchers)
  Includes index.
  ISBN 978-1-60270-729-0
  1. Thunderstorm—Juvenile literature. I. Ward, Damian, 1977- ill. II. Title.
  QC968.2.H54 2010
  551.55'4—dc22
                                                    2009029373

Table of Contents

A Dark Afternoon

It's afternoon, but the sky is very dark. Suddenly there's a flash of light! Then, *CRACK-BOOM-ba-boom-boom!*

But you are not scared. You know it's just a thunderstorm.

Thunderclouds are most common in spring and summer. They form late in the day when the air is warmest.

A Special Cloud

A thunderstorm comes from a special cloud. It is called a thundercloud. A thundercloud is dark gray. It stretches up into the sky. The top part of a thundercloud is called a thunderhead.

A thundercloud does not only make rain. It can also bring strong winds. It can drop hail. It can even create a tornado.

One thing about a thundercloud never changes. It always makes lightning and thunder.

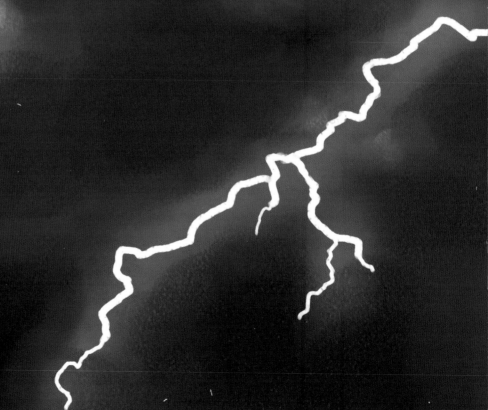

A typical thunderstorm lasts 30 minutes.

A thundercloud is
full of tiny water
droplets. There are
hailstones and tiny ice
crystals, too. Strong winds
blow everything around.
The droplets, hailstones,
and crystals crash
and bounce off
each other.

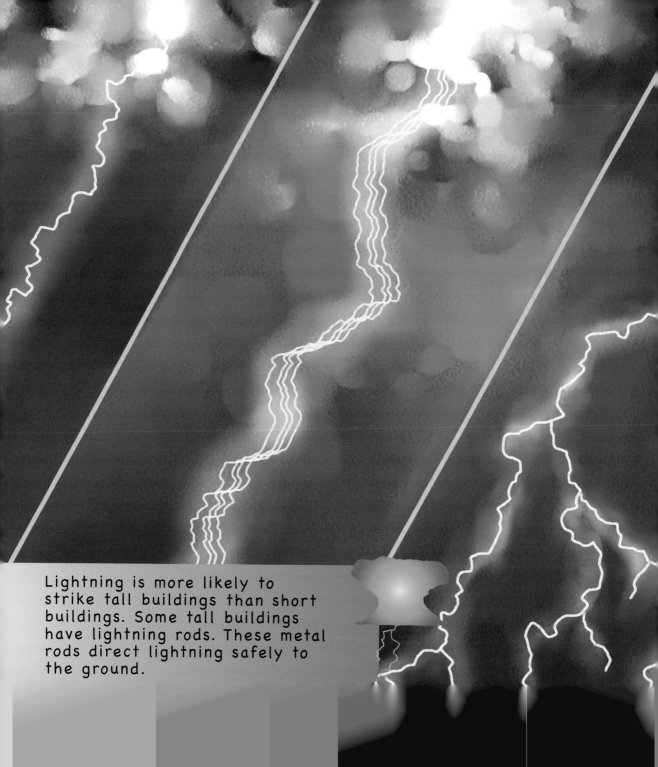

Lightning is more likely to
strike tall buildings than short
buildings. Some tall buildings
have lightning rods. These metal
rods direct lightning safely to
the ground.

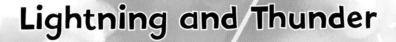

Lightning and Thunder

All that bouncing, crashing, and rubbing creates static electricity. An electric charge builds up inside the cloud. A huge spark jumps from the cloud. It's lightning! There are many different kinds of lightning.

14

Lightning travels through air. The air around it gets up to 50,000 degrees Fahrenheit (27,760°C). That is hotter than the surface of the sun. The air explodes. It makes a loud noise. It's thunder!

Tomorrow's Weather

Will there be a thunderstorm tomorrow? Scientists look at clues to find out. They look at how strong the wind is and which way the clouds are moving. They also look at how much water is in the air.

The weather report might include
a severe thunderstorm watch.
That means a strong thunderstorm
might be on the way. If the watch
changes to a severe thunderstorm
warning, a dangerous storm has
arrived. Take cover inside. Stay
away from windows.

Scientists use computers to put the clues together and make a weather forecast. Turn on the television or radio. See what the weather report says.

Will the game be rained out?

Stormy Earth

Thunderstorms bring needed rain for plants. But sometimes they bring too much rain. This causes floods. Floods can kill crops and damage houses.

Floods can even fill up city streets. One of the worst floods happened in 1972 in Rapid City, South Dakota.

Thunderstorms cause other problems, too. Lightning can knock over a tree. If the tree falls on a power line, the whole neighborhood could lose electricity. It might take hours for the electric company to fix it.

If you see a fallen power line, stay back! It is very dangerous. Call 911.

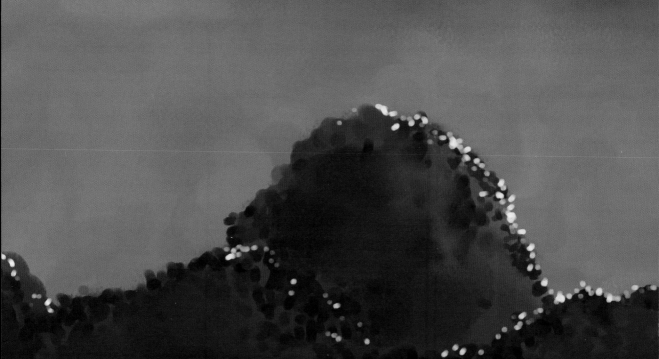

In the forest, lightning can make a tree go up in flames. If it is dry enough, the flames may spread from tree to tree. That could start a forest fire.

Forest fires are not always bad. A forest fire can be good for a forest that is overgrown.

Safely Inside

If a thunderstorm is coming, stay safe.
Get out of the water. You are safer inside
a car. But cars should not drive through
a flooded street. If the storm is severe,
go inside a house or building.

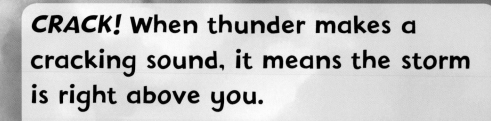

CRACK! When thunder makes a cracking sound, it means the storm is right above you.

Watch the lightning flash. Hear the thunder rumble. Enjoy some of Earth's most amazing weather.

Thunderstorms are Earth's most common weather event. There are about 2,000 thunderstorms happening right now.

How a Thunderstorm Forms

1. A giant thundercloud forms.

2. Inside the thundercloud, strong winds blow water droplets, hailstones, and ice crystals into each other.

3. The crashing inside the cloud causes static electricity. The static electricity causes a spark. Lightning flashes!

4. The air around the lightning gets super hot. Thunder booms!

Thunderstorm Facts

State by State
In the United States, Florida and parts of Colorado get more thunderstorms than any other state. Alaska, Washington, and Oregon get the fewest thunderstorms.

Angry Gods?
In ancient times, people did not know that lightning was an electric spark. Many societies believed that gods made lightning when they were angry.

The Stormiest
A town in Uganda, Africa, gets more thunderstorms than any other place on Earth. It has thunderstorms about 251 days of the year.

Glossary

flood — when large amounts of water flow onto areas that are normally dry, such as streets and fields.

forecast — a scientific guess about weather conditions in the coming days.

hailstones — chunks of ice that fall from thunderclouds.

static electricity — a kind of electricity that comes from certain materials rubbing against each other.

tornado — a tunnel of spinning wind that hangs from a thundercloud and destroys things in its path.

On the Web

To learn more about thunderstorms, visit ABDO Group online at **www.abdopublishing.com**. Web sites about thunderstorms are featured on our Book Links page. These links are routinely monitored and updated to provide the most current information available.

Index